Opposites

Old and New

Siân Smith

Heinemann
LIBRARY

Chicago, Illinois

© 2015 Heinemann Library
an imprint of Capstone Global Library, LLC
Chicago, Illinois

Edited by Siân Smith, Diyan Leake, and Brynn Baker
Designed by Tim Bond and Peggie Carley
Picture research by Elizabeth Alexander
Production by Victoria Fitzgerald
Originated by Capstone Global Library Ltd

Library of Congress Cataloging-in-Publication Data
ISBN 978-1-4846-0335-2 (paperback)
ISBN 978-1-4846-0350-5 (ebook PDF)

Acknowledgments
We would like to thank the following for permission to reproduce photographs: Alamy: milos luzanin, 14; Getty Images: ballyscanlon, 5, 22a, Dave King, 13, lina, aidukaite, 8, NI QIN, 10; Shutterstock: A_Belov, 16, Africa Studio, 17, Aleksandar Mijatovic, front cover right, Chamille White, 21 left, dinadesign, front cover left, drpnncpptak, 9, ljansempoi, 21 right, Irantzu Arbaizagoitia, 6, back cover bottom, Jjustas, 18, Kemeo, 20 left, Milos Luzanin, 12, restyler, 20 right, Sretnaz, 4, 22b, back cover top

Every effort has been made to contact copyright holders of material reproduced in this book. Any omissions will be rectified in subsequent printings if notice is given to the publisher.

Contents

Old and New

These socks are **old**.

These socks are **new**.

Are these socks old or new?

The socks are new.

This clock is old.

This clock is new.

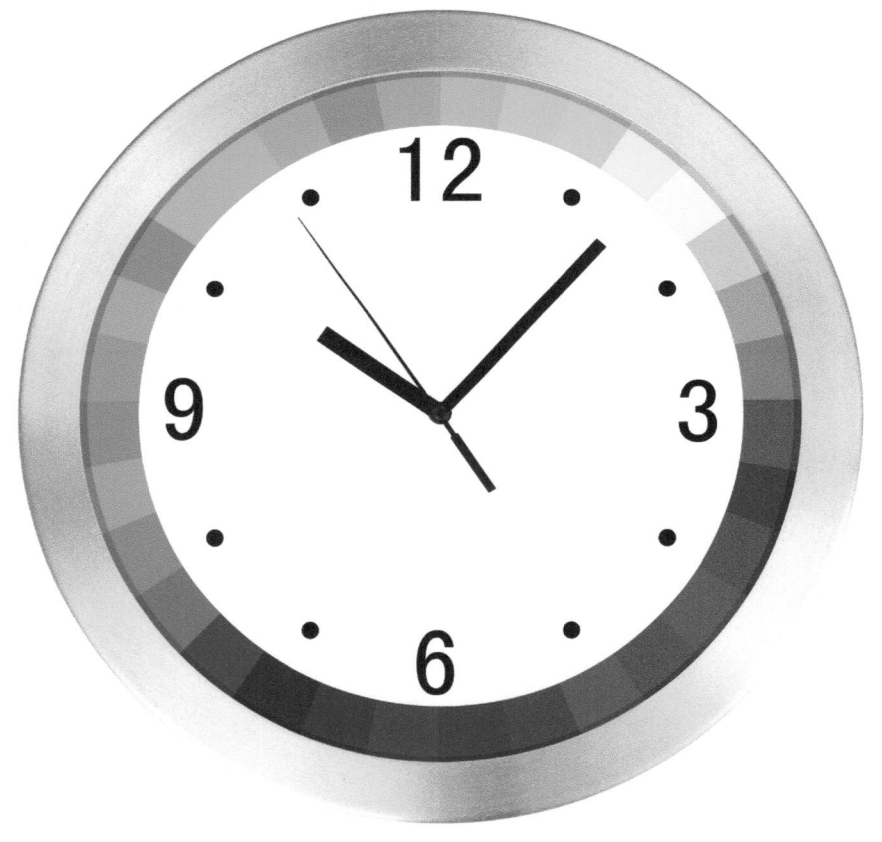

Is this clock old or new?

The clock is new.

The teddy bear is old.

The teddy bear is new.

Is this teddy bear old or new?

14

The teddy bear is old.

The book is old.

The book is new.

Is this book old or new?

18

The book is old.

Old and New Quiz

Which of these things are old?

Which of these things are new?

Answers on page 22

Picture Glossary

new just made or begun

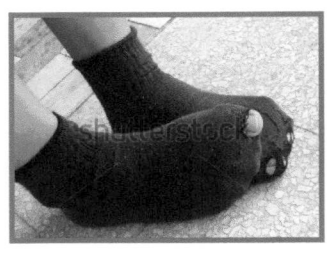

old has been used for a long time

Index

Answers to questions on pages 20 and 21

Left photo is old.

Right photo is new.

22

Notes for Teachers and Parents

BEFORE READING

Building background:

Ask children to think about something in their house that is new and something that is old.

AFTER READING

Recall and reflection:

Ask children if they like old or new things best. Do they like new clothes? New toys? Do they have some old toys that are their favorites? An old teddy bear or an old doll? Do we sometimes like old things best?

Sentence knowledge:

Help children find pages which have questions. How do they know?

Word knowledge (phonics):

Encourage children to point at the word *sock* on page 4. Sound out the three phonemes in the word *s/o/ck*. Ask children to sound out each phoneme as they point at the letters and then blend the sounds together to make the word *sock*. Challenge them to say some words that rhyme with *sock*. (clock, lock, knock, rock)

Word recognition:

Ask children to point at the word *book* on page 16.

AFTER-READING ACTIVITIES

Create a space on a bulletin board with a two-column chart with the columns labeled *Old* and *New*. Have children draw or cut out pictures of items both old and new to place on the display.

In This Book

Topic

old and new

Sentence stems

1. This is an old ___.
2. This ___ is new.
3. Is this ___ old or new?
4. This ___ is old.

High-frequency words

and

are

of

or

is

the

these

this

which

4

Table of Contents

Pebble Books are published by Capstone Press,
1710 Roe Crest Drive, North Mankato, Minnesota 56003
www.capstonepub.com

Library of Congress Cataloging-in-Publication Data
Cane, Ella.
Continents in my world / by Ella Cane.
pages cm. — (Pebble books. My world.)
Includes index.
ISBN 978-1-4765-3123-6 (library binding)
ISBN 978-1-4765-3465-7 (paperback)
ISBN 978-1-4765-3471-8 (ebook pdf)
1. Continents—Juvenile literature. I. Title.
GB423.C36 2013
910.914'1—dc23   2013005992

Summary: Simple text and full-color photographs introduce the continents of the
world to the reader.

Note to Parents and Teachers

The My World set supports national curriculum standards for
social studies related to people, places, and environments. This
book describes and illustrates continents. The images support
early readers in understanding the text. The repetition of words
and phrases helps early readers learn new words. This book
also introduces early readers to subject-specific vocabulary
words, which are defined in the Glossary section. Early readers
may need assistance to read some words and to use the Table
of Contents, Glossary, Read More, Internet Sites, and Index
sections of the book.

Pebble®

My World

Continents
in My World

by Ella Cane

Consulting Editor: Gail Saunders-Smith, PhD

T0052492

CAPSTONE PRESS
a capstone imprint

What Are Continents?

Earth is covered mostly by water. But there are huge pieces of land too. These landmasses are called continents.

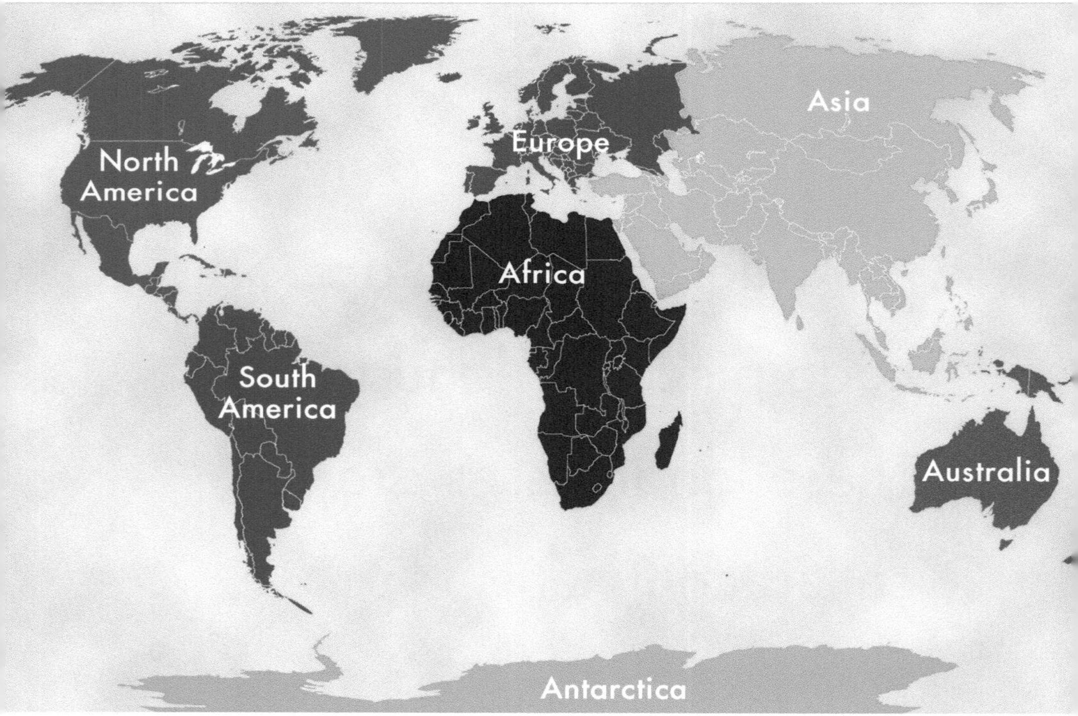

North America

Europe

Asia

Africa

South America

Australia

Antarctica

The world's seven continents are Asia, Africa, North America, South America, Antarctica, Europe, and Australia.

8

Asia

Asia is the largest continent on Earth. It also has the most people. More than 3.8 billion people live in Asia!

10

Africa

Africa is the second largest continent. It has the world's largest desert, the Sahara.

North America

North America is the third largest continent. Its Rocky Mountains are about 3,000 miles (4,828 kilometers) long.

South America

South America is Earth's fourth largest continent. The world's largest rain forest, the Amazon, is found there.

Antarctica

The fifth largest continent is Antarctica. It is where we find the South Pole. Antarctica is almost completely solid ice.

Europe

Europe is the sixth largest continent. The Alps stretch about 700 miles (1,127 km) across Europe.

Australia

The smallest continent is Australia. A large rock called Uluru lies in central Australia. Which continent would you like to visit?

Glossary

Alps—a large mountain range in Europe

Amazon rain forest—the largest tropical rain forest in the world; it covers northern South America

desert—a dry area with little rain

rain forest—a thick forest where rain falls nearly every day

Rocky Mountains—a large mountain range in western North America; also known as the Rockies

Sahara—the largest desert in the world; it covers most of northern Africa

South Pole—the southern-most point on Earth

Uluru—a large sandstone formation in central Australia that is about 1,142 feet (348 meters) tall; also known as Ayers Rock

Read More

Kalman, Bobbie. *The ABCs of Continents.* The ABCs of the Natural World. New York: Crabtree, 2009.

Mitten, Ellen. *Counting the Continents.* Little World Geography. Vero Beach, Fla.: Rourke Pub., 2009.

Schaefer, A. R. *Spotlight on Asia.* Spotlight on the Continents. Mankato, Minn.: Capstone Press, 2011.

Internet Sites

FactHound offers a safe, fun way to find Internet sites related to this book. All of the sites on FactHound have been researched by our staff.

Here's all you do:

Visit *www.facthound.com*

Type in this code: 9781476531236

Check out projects, games and lots more at
www.capstonekids.com

Index

Word Count: 159
Grade: 1
Early-Intervention Level: 16

Editorial Credits
Shelly Lyons, editor; Juliette Peters, designer; Marcie Spence, media researcher; Eric Manske, production specialist

Photo Credits
iStockphotos: Massimo Merlini, 20; Shutterstock: Anton Balazh, cover, Antonio S, 18, BartlomiejMagierowski, 8, Dr. Morley Read, 14, Galyna Andrushko, 10, Ieonello calvetti, 1, MarcelClemens, 4, Peter Kunasz, 12, Stawek, 6, Volodymyr Goinyk, 16